CONTENTS

iv Foreword
vi Acknowledgments

1   Introduction
3   Twenty-First-Century Statecraft
12 Institutional Reform: Seismic Culture Shifts Needed
23 Workforce: Open Pipeline, Revolving Door, and Minds
28 Beyond the Near Term
31 Conclusion

33 Endnotes
36 About the Authors
38 Advisory Committee

FOREWORD

Diplomacy is a critical tool in a nation's foreign policy tool kit, enabling a country to leverage its power and bring it to bear on critical international issues. The United States' most enduring advantage over its rivals is its unprecedented network of alliances, and through consultations officials and diplomats maintain these relationships and enlist allies in common causes. Those representing the government are tasked to negotiate treaties, dealing with issues from arms control to climate change, and advance U.S. interests in international organizations. They are the face of America overseas, representing the country around the world and providing critical services to Americans traveling abroad.

Too often, however, diplomacy is neglected. Sometimes serious diplomacy is sidelined in favor of unrealistic calls for regime change or demands that the other party cannot reasonably be expected to meet. A related problem, one highlighted by former Secretary of Defense Robert M. Gates, is that American foreign policy has become over-militarized, with the military asked to perform missions such as nation-building that it was never intended to. While the Department of Defense receives record appropriations, the Department of State struggles to have its comparatively small budget approved.

In this valuable and timely Council Special Report, Jon Finer, an adjunct senior fellow for U.S. foreign policy at the Council on Foreign Relations, and Uzra S. Zeya, the CEO and president of the Alliance for Peacebuilding, propose policies for revitalizing the State Department and American diplomacy. They rightly assess that the Department of State "has fallen into a deep and sustained period of crisis." They point out that the State Department is currently enduring turbulence but, equally important, that many of its problems are deep-seated and predate the Donald J. Trump administration. They provide an array

COUNCIL *on*
FOREIGN
RELATIONS

Council Special Report No. 89
November 2020

Revitalizing the State Department and American Diplomacy

Uzra S. Zeya and Jon Finer

The Council on Foreign Relations (CFR) is an independent, nonpartisan membership organization, think tank, and publisher dedicated to being a resource for its members, government officials, business executives, journalists, educators and students, civic and religious leaders, and other interested citizens in order to help them better understand the world and the foreign policy choices facing the United States and other countries. Founded in 1921, CFR carries out its mission by maintaining a diverse membership, with special programs to promote interest and develop expertise in the next generation of foreign policy leaders; convening meetings at its headquarters in New York and in Washington, DC, and other cities where senior government officials, members of Congress, global leaders, and prominent thinkers come together with Council members to discuss and debate major international issues; supporting a Studies Program that fosters independent research, enabling CFR scholars to produce articles, reports, and books and hold roundtables that analyze foreign policy issues and make concrete policy recommendations; publishing *Foreign Affairs*, the preeminent journal on international affairs and U.S. foreign policy; sponsoring Independent Task Forces that produce reports with both findings and policy prescriptions on the most important foreign policy topics; and providing up-to-date information and analysis about world events and American foreign policy on its website, CFR.org.

The Council on Foreign Relations takes no institutional positions on policy issues and has no affiliation with the U.S. government. All views expressed in its publications and on its website are the sole responsibility of the author or authors.

Council Special Reports (CSRs) are concise policy briefs, produced to provide a rapid response to a developing crisis or contribute to the public's understanding of current policy dilemmas. CSRs are written by individual authors—who may be CFR fellows or acknowledged experts from outside the institution—in consultation with an advisory committee, and are intended to take sixty days from inception to publication. The committee serves as a sounding board and provides feedback on a draft report. It usually meets twice—once before a draft is written and once again when there is a draft for review; however, advisory committee members, unlike Task Force members, are not asked to sign off on the report or to otherwise endorse it. Once published, CSRs are posted on CFR.org.

For further information about CFR or this Special Report, please write to the Council on Foreign Relations, 58 East 68th Street, New York, NY 10065, or call the Communications office at 212.434.9888. Visit our website, CFR.org.

To submit a letter in response to a Council Special Report for publication on our website, CFR.org, you may send an email to publications@cfr.org. Alternatively, letters may be mailed to us at: Publications Department, Council on Foreign Relations, 58 East 68th Street, New York, NY 10065. Letters should include the writer's name, postal address, and daytime phone number. Letters may be edited for length and clarity, and may be published online. Please do not send attachments. All letters become the property of the Council on Foreign Relations and will not be returned. We regret that, owing to the volume of correspondence, we cannot respond to every letter.

of policy proposals they believe the State Department can and should implement to restore American diplomacy.

The list of proposals is long, and few readers will agree with all of them. In some cases what is put forward will likely meet with bureaucratic or congressional resistance. What is clear and inarguable, though, is that U.S. foreign policy needs to better recognize and reflect the unique and valuable contributions of diplomacy. The State Department needs to rethink its organization along with the role of embassies and those who serve in them, attract individuals with more diverse backgrounds, skill sets, and experience, and reimagine career paths and training opportunities. The goal should be to attract the best and brightest to the State Department, be it for a career or a stint, and to invest in them so that those designing and carrying out American foreign policy have the creativity and professionalism required to meet the challenges and opportunities of a twenty-first-century world. All of which is to say that revitalizing the State Department should be a priority for the next administration regardless of who occupies the Oval Office.

Richard N. Haass
President
Council on Foreign Relations
November 2020

ACKNOWLEDGMENTS

This Council Special Report benefited and drew inspiration from many excellent reports and recommendations put forth over decades from institutions including the American Academy of Diplomacy, the American Foreign Service Association, the Atlantic Council, the Stimson Center, the U.S. Commission on Civil Rights, and the U.S. General Accountability Office. We also solicited input from an advisory committee comprising some of the nation's most experienced former Foreign and Civil Service officers and State Department political appointees from both parties. The advisory committee was led by Ambassadors William J. Burns and Linda Thomas-Greenfield, two of the most accomplished and respected career diplomats of their or any other generation and whose perspective was integral to the ambition and scope of this report. We are also grateful to our patient and tireless research associate Sherry Cho and to Joshua Rubin and Thomas Kagan, who provided additional support. Patricia Dorff and Katherine De Chant, from the Council's Publications team, provided thoughtful and incisive edits. We are also grateful to Council President Richard N. Haass and Senior Vice President and Director of Studies James M. Lindsay for approving and helping design this project.

With thanks to the institutions and individuals highlighted above, this report reflects our personal views and does not represent organizations with which we are affiliated.

Uzra S. Zeya
Jon Finer

INTRODUCTION

It has become an article of faith among policymakers that principled American leadership has waned but remains in demand around the world. Moreover, America's network of international relationships is its foremost strategic asset, even as the agency charged with advancing U.S. interests through diplomacy—the Department of State (DOS)—has fallen into a deep and sustained period of crisis. However, there is a third framing assumption: that the current crisis offers an opportunity to address this predicament and revitalize American diplomacy. Despite the decades-long failure to implement essential reforms—and even in the face of sustained hostility from the current administration—diplomacy remains the best tool the United States has to advance its foreign policy interests.

The role of the State Department has received heightened attention amid the onslaught it has suffered under the Donald J. Trump administration, which has treated American diplomats and diplomacy with a mix of neglect and disdain. But many of the challenges facing the DOS have existed for decades. Deficits in diversity, institutional culture, and professionalization are endemic to the State Department as an institution, and a diminished policy role for career officials persisted under previous administrations. Too often, leaders from both major parties have taken public support for U.S. leadership in the world for granted without making a strong enough case to the American public for why it is essential. Concrete steps can, and should, be taken solely through executive action in the first year of an administration committed to revitalizing American diplomacy, with thought to cementing change through legislation.

The most pressing challenges facing the State Department include a twenty-first-century policy environment that has, in some priority areas, evolved beyond the core competencies of most Foreign and Civil Service officers and an institution hollowed out by three years of talent flight, mired in excessively layered structure, and resistant to reform. Perhaps most important, they include the multigenerational challenge of a diplomatic workforce that falls woefully short of reflecting the diverse country it serves, particularly at the senior-most ranks, compromising its effectiveness and fostering a homogeneous and risk-averse culture that drives out rather than cultivates fresh perspectives. The State Department today risks losing the "war for talent," not only to the private sector but increasingly to other government agencies, due to inflexible career tracks, self-defeating hiring constraints, and a lack of commitment to training and professional development. Finally, DOS is hampered by Congress's failure over many years to pass authorizing legislation, leading to budgetary pressures and diminishing DOS's status in the hierarchy of national security agencies rather than reinforcing the nation's paramount foreign policy institution.

In an era in which the United States' military and economic advantages over its nearest rivals are eroding and the more than $5 trillion spent in the U.S. war on terrorism since 9/11 has corresponded with a fivefold increase in global terrorist attacks annually, alliances and relationships with partners around the world are ever-important components of U.S. national power.[1] In recent years, for a range of reasons, the United States' international relationships have atrophied along with its diplomatic capacity to leverage them against the threats and opportunities it faces. The profoundly challenging moment at home—interrelated crises of public health, economic prosperity, and racial justice—is all the more reason to take stock of how to participate in the wider world, not turn away from it.

But this situation can be reversed. The State Department's ranks are still among the most talented professional public servants anywhere in the government. When properly empowered and entrusted with significant responsibilities, American diplomats play essential roles in consequential outcomes for the country—from the Iran nuclear deal and Paris climate accord in the Barack Obama administration to the Afghanistan peace process and the release of American prisoners from various countries under President Trump. And its current predicament could make the State Department itself, which has long resisted fundamental reform, more open to badly needed changes. This report does not speak to every challenge the State Department faces but rather highlights the reform areas that we identified as reflecting greatest need based on discussions with veteran diplomats and other experts.

TWENTY-FIRST-CENTURY STATECRAFT

For diplomacy to remain the foremost tool of American foreign policy, the State Department should be appropriately postured against the range of emerging national security threats and opportunities the nation faces. In the era since 9/11, the United States came to rely more heavily on military force to pursue "forever wars" overseas, amid a bipartisan consensus that terrorism was the country's foremost threat. More recently, the rise of China and renewed aggression from Russia have spurred calls to refocus U.S. foreign policy on "great power conflict." Wherever the balance of emphasis lands in the coming decades between emerging national and transnational threats, both will be paramount to national security, as will the work of diplomats to address them.

The State Department should therefore develop—both within the Foreign and Civil Service and by bringing on board top outside practitioners—greater expertise in the range of issues that will be essential to American leadership in the twenty-first century. This will include both returning to the essentials of diplomatic tradecraft—grounded in doctrine, case studies, and professional education—and extending them to the areas that will define the State Department's work in the decades ahead. The objective, in all cases, is not to assemble expertise for its own sake nor to remake the State Department as the foremost government repository of technical expertise, for which other government entities are better equipped—though the scale between generalist and specialists too often tilts toward the former. Rather, the goal is to position DOS for the essential role of leading U.S. diplomacy and shaping outcomes globally on the country's most pressing concerns. The following critical areas, therefore, are intended to reflect not so much top policy priorities as issues that will shape the decades to come and for which DOS is currently inadequately postured.

CLIMATE CHANGE

Climate change is the planet's gravest existential threat, requiring urgent global cooperation. Traditionally, the State Department has played the leading role in negotiating international climate agreements, including the landmark 2015 Paris Agreement, the most ambitious climate agreement ever reached. Until 2017, that work was led by the office of the special envoy for climate change (SECC), in the Bureau of Oceans and International Environmental and Scientific Affairs. In 2017, however, the special envoy role was eliminated and the office renamed the Office of Global Change. The United States ceased playing what had been a leadership role in the global movement against climate change and later announced its intention to withdraw from the Paris accord. The concern previous studies have expressed about the proliferation of special envoys is valid, but, in this case, an urgent reversal is in order. Moreover, to put climate change at the center of American foreign policy and integrate this work with its core diplomatic relationships, DOS should

- restore the SECC office and designate its head the special presidential envoy for climate change, charged with not just negotiating international climate agreements but also overseeing their implementation, promoting greater ambition among counterpart nations, and coordinating an annual global climate change report with input from each regional bureau;

- staff the restored SECC office with experts in climate science, including by detailing scientists from other government agencies and short-term appointees from outside the U.S. government, and combine with regional experts from Foreign Service and Civil Service;

- design and establish, within the Foreign Service Institute (FSI) and in consultation with academic and policy experts, a mandatory climate change curriculum;

- ensure climate change expertise throughout DOS leadership staff (offices of the secretary, deputy, and undersecretary for political affairs) in each regional bureau and every embassy, ideally by providing relevant training for at least one officer in each country;

- send an early department-wide cable from the secretary of state officially elevating climate change to a core U.S. foreign policy interest and provide climate change background updates and talking points for all significant diplomatic efforts; and

- direct the SECC, the Policy Planning Staff, and the Bureau of Population, Refugees, and Migration to develop a strategy for addressing the plight of migrants driven from their homes by factors related to climate change.

PANDEMIC DISEASE

The State Department's Office of International Health and Biodefense (IHB) is charged with leading the department's diplomatic response to infectious disease outbreaks and the development of vaccines and therapeutics, raising awareness of health priorities, and engaging the private sector and civil society in pursuit of those objectives. However, the response to the COVID-19 pandemic—which has already killed more Americans more quickly than any disease since the 1918 influenza pandemic—has illustrated how quickly diplomacy and the State Department's role can be marginalized in the event of a major global pandemic, despite the need for a coordinated diplomatic response. While overseas missions toiled to repatriate more than one hundred thousand Americans stranded abroad, DOS global policy response was limited to little more than occasional statements lashing out at China for its role in the initial outbreak.

Rather than collaborate with European and Asian allies and shape outcomes at international organizations such as the World Health Organization, the Trump administration has often been at odds with partners, even competing with them over procurement of essential personal protective equipment. The value of a concerted diplomatic and scientific response to pandemics is illustrated by the extraordinary work of the President's Emergency Plan for AIDS Relief (PEPFAR), launched by President George W. Bush in 2003. One of the most successful government programs in American history, PEPFAR achieved such strong bipartisan funding that it brought antiretroviral treatment to nearly fifteen million people worldwide. During the 2014 Ebola outbreak, after public health officials warned that upward of a million people could be killed worldwide, the State Department helped lead and coordinate an international public health response that kept the final death toll at just over ten thousand. The State Department should draw lessons from those experiences by

- better integrating expertise at the Department of Health and Human Services, Centers for Disease Control and Prevention, National Institutes of Health, and U.S. Agency for International Development (USAID) with diplomatic acumen at IHB and DOS to formulate forward-leaning, preventive pandemic policies;

- prioritizing, within certain embassies, coordination with local public health officials to develop an early warning system in the event of an outbreak of infectious disease with pandemic potential;

- staffing IHB with experts in infectious disease epidemiology, including by detailing scientists from other government agencies and short-term appointees from outside the U.S. government; and

- officially elevating pandemic disease to a core U.S. national interest.

A GLOBAL DIPLOMATIC FOOTPRINT THAT MATCHES SHIFTING GLOBAL POWER

The end of the post-9/11 era and the rise of new challenges and opportunities around the world are ideal inflection points for the State Department to reexamine its global footprint to match resources with priorities. This realignment should begin with expanding DOS presence in Asia, home to most of the world's population, the largest share of global economic growth, and paramount security threats. Such an effort should go beyond past efforts—such as the 2006–09 Global Repositioning Initiative, which transferred more than three hundred Foreign Service overseas positions principally to China and India—to examine the totality of U.S. government presence abroad, including in rising powers and contested markets from Africa to the Western Hemisphere. More than any other foreign policy issue, the U.S.-China relationship has produced a nearly bipartisan consensus over the need to shift from the relatively collaborative and sanguine view of China's rise that characterized decades of American foreign policy to a more competitive, even confrontational, approach.

Presidents Obama and Trump both, to varying degrees, put China at the center of their worldview: Obama by seeking to "rebalance"

American resources and focus toward East Asia and Trump by embarking on an unprecedented trade conflict with Beijing. For the rest of this century, no matter which party is in power and what strategic approach it chooses, China will be at the center of American foreign policy. Other regional policy priorities outside the post-9/11 areas of focus will include India, the world's largest democracy; Southeast Asia, a bastion of global economic growth; the Western Hemisphere, home to America's primary trading partners and the source of a migration and humanitarian crisis and a policy crisis at the U.S.-Mexico border; and Nigeria, Africa's most populous country and largest economy, on pace to become the world's second most populous country by the end of this century. In order to manage these strategic relationships and advise policymakers, the State Department should adapt accordingly. This will mean

- conducting a global review of the number of U.S. government personnel, including from other agencies, in each diplomatic post and setting a goal of better matching personnel numbers to interest-based priorities within four years;

- increasing recruitment of both native Chinese speakers and students enrolled in top East Asian studies programs throughout the United States;

- designing Bureau of Intelligence and Research briefings on designated regional priorities and integrating them into consultations for every outgoing and incoming ambassador and public diplomacy officers destined abroad; and

- incentivizing—including with regard to promotion—Foreign Service officer (FSO) tours in or focused on China, as well as Chinese-language proficiency.

ECONOMIC COMPETITIVENESS, EQUITY, AND ANTICORRUPTION

The mission of the Bureau of Economic and Business Affairs (EB) is to "ensure the United States remains the world's strongest and most dynamic economy."[2] Yet, even though as many as forty million American jobs depend on trade, the State Department as a whole has rarely prioritized commercial diplomacy. To some extent, this could be the legacy of an era in which the United States represented upward of 40 percent of global gross domestic product. But with that number now cut in half and China set to surpass the U.S. economy in absolute size late this century, the mission of commercial advocacy—performed in overseas missions by both FSOs and the Commerce Department's Foreign Commercial Service—has never been more important.

Today, Chinese commercial diplomats dramatically outnumber their American counterparts in vital overseas markets and other major economies, including U.S. allies in East Asia and Western Europe. EB's mission should also be updated to address two shifting priorities. First, it should transcend the artificial barrier between domestic and foreign economic policy—for example, ensuring that the increasing focus on economic equity, not just growth, is reflected in overseas advocacy. Second, it should make fighting corruption in essential countries a foreign policy priority, given its strong resonance among populations around the world and documented link to instability, poor governance, and the rise of extremism. To remedy this deficit, DOS should

- require every U.S. ambassador, in conjunction with the country team and other U.S. government stakeholders, to write a business plan for how to advance the interests of American companies and submit it to the EB assistant secretary;

- direct EB to coordinate more closely with domestic and economic policy officials in the White House and other agencies, to ensure alignment between international and domestic economic priorities;

- establish anticorruption as a strategic priority and charge EB and the secretary of state's Policy Planning Staff with developing a department-wide approach to addressing this issue;

- provide more opportunities and career-enhancing incentives for Foreign and Civil Service officers to do time-limited secondments with American companies that have a significant overseas presence, as well as with other U.S. government agencies with an economic focus;

- implement the American Foreign Service Association's call for three hundred economic officers to be deployed overseas;

- make successful commercial participation and anticorruption part of the presidential letter of instruction to chiefs of mission, mandatory training for outgoing ambassadors, and annual employee evaluation reviews for senior FSOs and economic officers;

- bring experienced international business professionals into EB on time-limited assignments to lend their expertise to commercial advocacy efforts (ensuring a strict recusal from any issues of direct relevance to their employer);

- work with the Commerce Department and the International Development Finance Corporation to enhance American economic competitiveness and increase the number of commercial diplomats in critical markets; and

- clarify and strengthen guidelines around conflicts of interest for State Department personnel.

TECHNOLOGICAL TRANSFORMATION

DOS is in dire need of a technological overhaul, in terms of both the technology diplomats employ to do their jobs and the level of expertise in technology and cybersecurity policy. With regard to the former, nothing substitutes for public and private diplomacy conducted face to face with foreign audiences and counterparts, and the core mission of the State Department will always be that critical work. But long before the COVID-19 pandemic, the basic work of diplomacy had begun to change in response to new technologies and modes of communication, and DOS has done far too little to keep up. Too few officers have access to classified communications even in an office setting (and far fewer to the most secure, top secret email system). Virtually none are able to communicate securely while in transit.

Diplomats in Washington and the field have wide-ranging competency with, and employment of, social media. As the entire world moves to adopt videoconferencing in response to diminished travel and fewer large gatherings in the wake of the COVID-19 pandemic, the State Department will need the technology platforms and training to keep up. Meanwhile, the information environment in which foreign affairs are conducted is awash in technology-enabled disinformation, interference with U.S. and other countries' domestic politics, the imperative to build a consensus on international rules that will govern cyberspace, and an assault on fundamental truth that begins in the virtual world but does not remain there; these challenges have been exacerbated by the recent infrequency of what were once daily DOS press briefings.

The State Department's Global Engagement Center (GEC), charged with countering disinformation and computational propaganda, suffers from a lack of mission clarity, weak interagency standing, and inattention from DOS senior ranks, which sometimes leave it disconnected from policy priorities and outperformed by the better-funded propaganda operations of foreign rivals. The 2020 creation of a Center for Analytics and appointment of a chief data officer are promising steps toward filling a critical gap in American diplomacy, which remains woefully behind on machine learning, forecasting, and artificial intelligence tools to mine the trove of information and analysis generated by DOS personnel on twentieth-century platforms. To enhance a State Department that today is fundamentally ill-equipped for this modern digital landscape, DOS should

- review recommendations by experts in information technology to reform the department's technological platforms, pursue secure and cost-effective enhancements, and secure communications from inside and outside the government;

- increase opportunities for FSOs and specialists to do time-limited secondments and apprenticeships with American information and communications technology companies to develop relevant skills and reimagine their work;

- appoint a chief technology officer reporting directly to the secretary of state with private-sector, enterprise-wide executive experience, and direct them to build a "digital service corps" of short-term appointees from outside DOS embedded in each bureau to advise top diplomats on issues of technology and cybersecurity policy;

- elevate the DOS coordinator for cyber issues to the level of ambassador-at-large and charge the office with working alongside regional bureaus to build consensus on global norms and rules governing cyberspace;

- request a National Security Council–led process to rationalize and coordinate a government-wide strategy for the information environment, clarifying the missions and authorities of the GEC, the Department of

Defense, the intelligence community, and the various entities overseen by the U.S. Agency for Global Media; and

- resume the daily press briefings by the DOS spokesperson, to ensure that foreign policy positions are being clearly communicated to the nation and around the world in the increasingly contested information space.

INSTITUTIONAL REFORM
Seismic Culture Shifts Needed

No matter how many new Foreign and Civil Service officers are hired or how much funding for the International Affairs Account is increased, asserting State Department leadership in shaping a disrupted world will not be possible without seismic culture shifts within the institution. This means decisive and long-overdue action to make the State Department a diverse, equitable, and inclusive institution as trend lines accelerate in the opposite direction. Institutional transformation also requires moving away from an ingrained risk-aversion mindset, careerism, bureaucratic layering that tangles the Washington decision-making process, and hyper-politicization of diplomacy that has inflamed perennial political appointee-career divides, hollowed out senior career ranks, and tanked employee morale and recruitment numbers.

DIVERSITY AS A NATIONAL SECURITY PRIORITY

Although the greatest challenge for DOS leadership may be revitalizing a workforce pummeled by four years of unprecedented politicization and marginalization, perhaps the greatest deficit within that workforce remains its profound lack of diversity. Despite well-intentioned recruitment efforts such as the Pickering and Rangel fellowships, DOS has failed thus far to foster a Foreign Service that looks like America and is in fact reversing course with respect to African American and women's representation, especially at the uppermost levels. At a moment of domestic and global outcry over systemic anti-Black racism in the United States, exactly five African American ambassadors (only one of whom is a woman) serve overseas. For context, in their respective first terms Presidents Obama and Bush nominated twenty-three and nineteen Black ambassadors, of whom twenty-two total were women.

The State Department's public defensiveness in addressing diversity gaps often consists of selective data use, such as pointing to entry-level numbers while ignoring the crisis at the top or using the historically strong representation of African Americans in the Civil Service (which is declining, according to a 2020 Government Accountability Office [GAO] report) to suggest "nothing to see here."[3] With the State Department's African American workforce concentrated in lower-level Civil Service clerical and administrative jobs, the Foreign Service remains a bastion of white male privilege. The diversity deficit is most acute in the Senior Foreign Service, from which ambassadors and other career leadership are drawn, which is whiter in 2020 than in 2002. As of March 2020, the Senior Foreign Service was 90 percent white and 69 percent male, with the proportion of African American senior officers below 3 percent.[4] By comparison, 2008 State Department data showed the proportion of African American Senior Foreign Service officers at nearly 9 percent.

Although the proportion of women in the Foreign Service has increased incrementally over eighteen years, from 33 percent in 2002 to 35 percent today, this figure lags far behind a U.S. civilian labor force that is 48 percent women. Fiscal year 2019 Foreign Service workforce data shows men dominant at every rank, with the 60 percent male FS-01 (highest rank below Senior Foreign Service) cadre jumping to 70 percent at the FE-OC (lowest rank of Senior Foreign Service) level. The proportion of female Foreign Service specialists has dropped 10 percentage points since 1990, a trend DOS attributes to increased numbers for security officers, who were 90 percent male as of 2019.[5] The Trump administration reversed a twenty-five-plus-year trend of increasing the proportion of female ambassadors representing the United States abroad, down to 28 percent in 2020 from 33 percent throughout the Obama administration.

Although the State Department does not publish data on the numbers of Pickering and Rangel fellows who have left the Foreign Service at the entry or mid-level, former officers in this category who resigned to pursue successful careers in the tech, corporate, and nonprofit sectors have recounted a lack of support, in the form of mentoring and accompaniment, once fellows join Foreign Service ranks, as well as a rigid career track that often withholds greater responsibility until fifteen years in and makes it difficult for two-career couples to live and work in the same place. Others have spoken of pervading insensitivity to the racism that diplomats of color encounter overseas and recommended training to help prepare officers for hostility they could face abroad. Some report veiled to outright bias from U.S. government colleagues, from LGBTQ+ officers facing derogatory comments to women of color having their authority questioned by male officers who report to them or having older, white male supervisors chide them for "moving up too quickly."[6]

Given the setbacks of the last three years and insufficient progress of decades prior, achieving a Foreign Service that looks like America will not be possible within the rigidities of a thirty-year career track. Bold action is required to open the State Department workforce beyond the entry level now, through committing to achieve before 2030 a Foreign Service workforce, at all levels, in line with representation of women and persons of color in the general American population. With a vast body of research also showing that more diverse organizations are more innovative and effective, recognizing the State Department's diversity deficit as a national security risk is long overdue, as is undertaking five corrective measures, all within the secretary of state's existing legal authorities, as urgent, strategic priorities:

• Open career entry pipelines at all levels, heeding the advice of a 1989 GAO report that recommended numeric targets "for hiring and advancement by race, ethnic origin, and gender" to correct underrepresentation of women and minorities from entry to senior levels that persists thirty-plus years later; reestablish mid-level entry and make senior-level appointments up to a threshold of 5 percent of Senior Foreign Service numbers, with requisite training and accompaniment to ensure professional success; and aggressively use existing recall and reappointment authorities to bring back former FSOs up to the senior level with the energy, skills, experience, and diversity most needed at this moment.[7] Opening pipelines on a targeted basis at the mid- and senior levels also will serve to open the Foreign Service to diverse candidates with more substantial professional and international experience who are less inclined to start at the bottom to pursue a diplomatic career. A shift in recruiting beyond the entry level, similar to direct commissions in the U.S. military, would help the State Department redress more expeditiously and strategically the twenty-first-century statecraft gaps identified in the previous section, while shoring up core competencies, such as political-military affairs and public diplomacy.

- Prioritize diverse candidates and gender parity in senior appointments, learning from UN Secretary-General António Guterres's leadership push for gender parity throughout the UN system, starting at the senior level, accompanied by fixed deadlines and temporary special measures to accelerate progress;[8] embrace initiatives such as the Leadership Council for Women in National Security's call for gender parity in national security appointments, with prioritized attention to persons (including men) of color; and direct attention toward diversifying bureaus such as East Asian and Pacific Affairs, European and Eurasian Affairs, Western Hemisphere Affairs, and Near Eastern Affairs and breaking precedent of all-male ambassadorial nominees to large, high-priority missions such as Afghanistan, China, Germany, Israel, Russia, Saudi Arabia, and Turkey.

- Close the data gap by producing, publishing, analyzing, and acting on diversity statistics with respect to embassies, bureaus, position, and actual numbers, with prioritized attention to ambassadorships and positions at the deputy assistant secretary level and above; address lower promotion rates for racial minorities relative to whites in both the Foreign and the Civil Service, as well as the drop-off of women in the Senior Foreign Service relative to lower ranks, trends highlighted in the 2020 GAO report;[9] study retention of Pickering and Rangel fellows and reasons for their leaving service; and publish exit interview analysis for all State Department employees, with special attention to women and minorities.

- Increase accompaniment to support retention, elevating mentoring as a requirement for senior officers and those seeking promotion to senior levels; increase funding and senior leadership support for employee-run affinity groups long operating on a voluntary basis; train diverse employees about bias they could encounter in overseas environments and how to address it; commit leadership to secure visas for same-sex spouses of

LGBTQ+ employees serving abroad who face more limited prospects for worldwide assignment; and expand opportunities and flexibility for overseas spousal employment.

- Revise promotion precepts to hold officers, bureaus, and embassies accountable for fostering more diverse, inclusive, and equitable workplaces; use data to measure and reward progress and counteract indifference; move beyond a long-articulated zero tolerance of sexual harassment and bias to ensure swift disciplinary action for offenders, including dismissal of those found to have committed even one confirmed incident of harassment or bias; create an employee commission to monitor harassment complaints and propose institutional reform; and increase support mechanisms for survivors of sexual harassment and abuse, especially locally employed staff who lack recourse to the U.S. equal employment opportunity system and are more vulnerable in overseas environments.

Executing this five-part agenda requires top-level ownership and accountability as well. Responsibility for closing the diversity gap will be in the hands of the director general (DG), reporting to the undersecretary for management, in turn accountable to the deputy secretary of state, who can ensure bureau-wide action and promote the culture shifts needed to do so. The secretary of state should require a concrete plan in the first six months on how the DG will ramp up action, with benchmarks.

OVERCOMING RISK-AVERSION CULTURE

Beyond the diversity gap but perhaps not unrelated to it, a diverse range of former career and noncareer officers identified overcoming a prevailing culture of risk aversion as one of the State Department's most serious challenges. This reality manifests itself both externally, in the form of "fortress embassies" and increased difficulty engaging local populations even in non–high threat environments, and internally, with respect to a "don't make waves" approach to career advancement.

As Ambassador Anne Patterson wrote in 2019,

> Our aversion to risk means that we know less—in fact, we are blind in critical countries. So we made mistakes in Libya, in Egypt and in Saudi Arabia, because we did not have a good understanding of the local scene.

Fundamentally, the State Department has become profoundly reluctant to put people in harm's way, under any circumstances. And because we are not on the ground in places like northeastern Syria or Libya or Yemen, we have turned more and more of the responsibility over to the Department of Defense. Further, unpredictable withdrawals of personnel and closing of embassies make us look afraid; and that, too, has long-term consequences.[10]

This challenge is more rooted in politics than security realities, epitomized by the partisan firestorm and more than a dozen investigations following the September 2012 attacks in Benghazi that killed four Americans and further ingrained the risk-aversion mindset at DOS. Experience from Afghanistan to Libya shows that, once a U.S. diplomatic mission is closed, it can take years, if not decades, to reestablish a U.S. presence.

The post-9/11 surge in unaccompanied Foreign Service positions at overseas posts—which saw a fivefold increase from 2003 to 2013 and remains at fifteen to twenty diplomatic posts a year—reflects a long-term reality with which the State Department has yet to fully come to grips.[11] Rather than filling positions through incentive packages rooted in careerism and expedience—preferential next assignments, danger bonuses, shorter tours—the State Department needs to take a hard look at what is being accomplished strategically when personnel do not leave compounds, lack expertise in the countries in question, and remain on the ground for less than a year. One former FSO commented, "The proliferation of one-year postings are a disaster. They lead to morale problems, work imbalances, and vacancies."[12] The answer is not to pull up stakes entirely or cut positions without linkage to foreign policy outcomes sought, nor is it to take refuge in the status quo.[13] Many of these vexing questions remain unresolved eight years after the Benghazi attacks. One necessary step, amid a national consensus against "forever wars," is for the State Department to rethink its top-heavy approach to stabilization and expeditionary diplomacy shaped by nearly two decades of Iraq and Afghanistan staffing models that failed to deliver intended results. A revitalized DOS should eschew nation-building in favor of smart power approaches that prioritize conflict prevention and empower local partners and civil society actors to solve problems and build accountable institutions. This requires diplomatic agility to build coalitions, thwart spoilers, and bring armed conflicts to a negotiated end.

A distinct but related internal risk aversion is baked into a hierarchical system that positions FSOs in a near-perpetual hunt for their next assignment, decisions that often seem to boil down to who you know rather than what you have done. Getting a less-than-stellar review or alienating someone higher up can mean a career stalled or a dream assignment dashed. Keeping one's head down is for many the preferred course of action, one evident in the degree to which most senior career State Department officials acquiesced when colleagues were politically targeted, removed, or blocked from positions since 2017.

The "keep your head down" culture prevalent at DOS needs a reboot to "I have your back." Institutions such as the U.S. Marine Corps teach moral courage alongside physical courage, the former taking on greater importance and defined as staying true to one's integrity and the values of the institution. Current DOS senior leadership promotion precepts make no mention of moral courage, which is relegated to an entry-level managerial skill. Secretary Mike Pompeo's new ethos similarly makes no mention of risk-taking or moral courage, and the Quadrennial Diplomacy and Development Review initiated under the Obama administration did not lead to measurable change.[14]

Although courageous Foreign and Civil Service officers defying expediency or danger to advance American national security or uphold American values are not in short supply, they are not adequately reflected in those rising to the State Department's highest positions in Washington. The secretary of state should

- articulate greater risk tolerance and moral courage as the core of a necessary culture shift, offer political top-cover to institutionalize within their senior leadership team and DOS as a whole, and manage with Congress;

- designate the undersecretary for management to serve as the chief operating officer of the State Department, with a focus on fostering a culture of risk tolerance and innovation, linking resources and staffing to strategy, and closing the State Department's gaping diversity gap;

- commission a study to examine unaccompanied post policies and new measures to mitigate risk while allowing for more effective diplomatic efforts, to incentivize longer tours and offer greater duty of care to employees and families before, during, and after assignment;

- reach beyond senior DOS leadership to elevate career employees who have modeled leadership in challenging the status quo and accomplished U.S. national security goals in difficult and dangerous environments; and

- regularly brief House and Senate Foreign Affairs Committees on security plans for high-threat posts, to invest them in sharing associated risks.

DELAYERING AND DECENTRALIZING DECISION-MAKING

An agile, risk-tolerant, and morally courageous State Department needs a decision-making process to match. Deficits in this area long predate the current administration. As one former senior FSO commented, "The State Department has a lousy reputation of being effective policy players; we get in our own way."[15] The general culprit here is bureaucratic layering, embodied in a proliferation of bureaus and senior officials and accompanying "clearance hell" that can easily require a policy recommendation to obtain fifteen or more sign-offs before reaching the secretary of state's office. The process for sending instructions to embassies in the field is equally onerous and outdated, such that emails or phone calls often take the place of so-called front channel cables that can arrive after action is required.

Clearance reform efforts have come and gone for three decades. A completely new approach is now needed. This means replacing the current system with an agile policy coordination framework that allows for rapid synthesis and distillation of DOS and field expertise into cogent policy recommendations for principals, rigorous and transparent implementation once decisions are made, and more autonomy for embassies in the field. This requires clear articulation of the State Department's mission and policy decisions, designation of leads among bureaus and undersecretaries by DOS leadership, adoption of a more task force approach that transcends bureau lines, and more leadership from embassies in the field, where the greatest expertise on the countries in question lies. A transparent process would allow for multiple perspectives to be heard rather than paper over differences, such as by allowing bureaus to see each other's recommendations to the secretary of state and submit rebuttals. Such a process would also require better top-down information sharing, as even under the Obama administration written readouts of calls or meetings by the secretary of state could take weeks to reach action officers or embassies abroad or, in the case of the president, never arrive at all.

Although the amended Foreign Service Act allows up to six undersecretaries at the State Department, the undersecretary system and its organization are one more impediment to the State Department speaking with one voice. Multiple undersecretaries or their staffs should not be involved on the same policy issues. Reducing the number of undersecretaries, with bureaus allocated underneath them at the discretion of the incoming secretary of state, would help eliminate overlapping responsibilities, empower assistant secretaries and equivalents (such as the counselor and director of policy planning), and reduce layering while leaving sufficient senior management capacity in place. For similar reasons, the deputy secretary for management and resources, whose oversight functions can be handled by the deputy secretary of state and the undersecretary for management, should not be restored. Further changes should include reducing top-level staff numbers, empowering assistant secretaries who in turn would delegate responsibility to a smaller subset of deputy assistant secretaries and down the chain to give a more meaningful experience to DOS employees who would normally have to wait fifteen years or more for supervisory responsibility. The impetus is strong for decentralization in the form of a leaner DOS and more Foreign Service positions overseas, where the work has greater effect and gaps are more detrimental to U.S. national security. Reduction of Foreign Service positions in Washington could also give more mobility opportunities to Civil Service employees who are stifled in an antiquated personnel system with insufficient paths for advancement or professional development.

Other ways to correct the imbalance between Washington and the field would be to delegate more authority overseas, as the Defense Department does with combatant commands, and give chiefs of mission more authority over their budgets, hiring, and oversight of other agencies in the field, which can often outnumber the State Department presence at post. The Washington-field imbalance is borne out by 2018 State Department workforce planning data, which found that 11 percent of overseas Foreign Service positions were vacant and 32 percent of the Foreign Service was assigned domestically.[16]

To address these issues, the secretary of state should

- optimize State Department decision-making through a streamlined alternative to the paper clearance system;

- reduce the number of undersecretaries and delegate more authority to empowered assistant secretaries and equivalents and ambassadors in the field; and

- correct the imbalance between Washington and the field by rebalancing Foreign Service positions overseas according to strategic needs and giving more opportunities and training for Civil Service employees to fill policy positions in Washington.

RESTORING TRUST AND BRIDGING THE CAREER-NONCAREER DIVIDE

Fostering a culture of risk-taking and innovation will require bridging a perennial trust gap between political appointees and career employees that has become a chasm in recent years.

The effects of this phenomenon on State Department morale, capacity, and recruitment have been staggering. From 2014 to 2019, the State Department fell ten rungs in the Best Places to Work in Government survey, from third to thirteenth. Between October 2017 and October 2018, 8,685 people signed up to take the FSO test, a 22 percent decline relative to the previous year and the lowest number of test applicants since 2008.[17]

Even more glaring than the decline in State Department morale and recruiting numbers is the near-elimination of senior career leadership at the assistant secretary level and higher. With the exception of the director general for human resources, a non-policymaking role mandated by law to be a career senior FSO, no active-duty career assistant secretary leads any department bureau administration. The proportion of political appointee ambassadors, meanwhile, is at a modern-day high, 43 percent, relative to an average of about 31 percent from the Jimmy Carter through Barack Obama administrations. While non-career ambassadors can bring fresh ideas, leadership acumen, and political cachet to a bilateral relationship, the long-standing, bipartisan practice of rewarding donors with plum postings undercuts U.S. national security as well as career officer advancement and sets the United States apart from most of its allies, China, and Russia.

Factor in the serial removal of accomplished deputy chiefs of mission by political appointee ambassadors and nonresponses to cases of political retaliation and bias by senior appointees, and the result is a sense of a Civil and Foreign Service under siege.[18] To restore trust with a beleaguered career cadre, the secretary of state and White House should

- restore primacy of career expertise in senior appointments, including more than 50 percent of DOS positions above the assistant secretary level and more than 75 percent of ambassadorial nominations;

- prioritize diverse candidates and commit to gender parity in senior appointments;

- appoint career ambassadors to the committee that recommends ambassadorial nominations, to involve more career leaders in a process dominated by noncareer appointees;

- require all incoming noncareer appointees to undergo training in leadership, management, and Washington tradecraft; and

- issue a public apology for career employees subjected to political retaliation, redress the adverse effects on their careers and personal welfare, and ensure accountability and personnel protections to prevent a recurrence.

WORKFORCE
Open Pipeline, Revolving Door, and Minds

With more than half of Foreign and Civil Service employees having less than ten years of experience, domestic Civil Service staffing frozen at 2017 levels, and a brain drain of senior talent since 2017, urgent attention needs to be devoted to revitalizing the professional path and retention of the current DOS workforce.[19] The State Department's lack of transparency on how many employees it has lost since 2017 makes a damage assessment difficult. American Foreign Service Association data from December 2016 through December 2018 suggest a decimation of DOS senior ranks: a loss of fourteen career ministers (three-star general equivalents), ninety-four minister counselors (two-star equivalents), and sixty-eight counselors (one-star equivalents)—22 percent of the roughly eight hundred–strong Senior Foreign Service.[20] More information is needed with respect to losses at the critical 01 level on the cusp of entry to senior ranks.

Mindful of the sensitivity of career officers who advanced national security under significant hardship under the Trump administration, a "right of return" within limits would be beneficial, focused on those who left the State Department in the last ten years and who have the requisite moral courage, leadership and management skills, and expertise in essential policy areas to augment the institution at this critical moment. Special attention should be paid to entrepreneurial former mid-level officers with private and nongovernmental sector leadership acumen who can lead the cultural and institutional shifts elaborated earlier in this report. These officers should come in at the rank reflecting their current skill level, not the rank at which they left the State Department.

Recruitment, assignments, and advancement systems created fifty years ago have questionable relevance for generations for whom a twenty-five-year career track is an anachronism. Delayering and delegating authority down will give officers more responsibility earlier.[21] Studies such as the 2018 American Academy of Diplomacy report "Strengthening the Department of State" and the 2017 Atlantic Council "Roadmap for State Department Reform" offer detailed and worthy recommendations for supporting a more agile and able Foreign Service generalist, specialist, and Civil Service workforce. In addition, a leadership-driven, employee-led effort should examine the following:

- replacing or offering alternative entry paths to the FSO written examination and oral examination processes, which focus on weeding out unsuccessful candidates rather than recruiting the most talented ones

- further streamlining the Foreign Service evaluation process, which takes an inordinate quarter of the calendar year away from achievement of national security goals

- replacing the competitive bidding process, which fuels careerism and risk aversion, with a more directed, portfolio approach to Foreign Service assignments that builds skills, develops talent and expertise, and meets DOS strategic needs, especially diversity

- revising or replacing the Foreign Service "cones" system to create more flexible career paths and meet twenty-first-century statecraft priorities

- increasing limited noncareer appointments with specialized expertise for shorter-term public service options

- creating more flexible paths for entry and advancement in the Civil Service, including cross-bureau mobility and overseas rotations that support professional development, surge, and vacancy needs

- reducing the number of overseas positions that can be done in Washington or by local staff, such as management, logistics, and back-office IT support

- extending overseas tours of duty to three to five years to deliver a greater return on investment and anchor greater continuity and expertise on the ground

- enabling the return of FSOs who left DOS in the past decade, performed at high level while in service, and accumulated relevant managerial experience or policy-relevant skills

A career path that gives both Civil and Foreign Service officers the opportunity to build skills outside DOS and strengthen the institution upon return would be valuable. The State Department has made useful strides by recently offering employees the option for three years' leave without pay, but a more intentional effort is in order to develop greater expertise in the areas DOS needs it most. The military does this effectively with congressional fellowships, interagency and White House details, and work at think tanks—assignments seen as opportunities that groom people for leadership positions. By contrast, former Foreign and Civil Service officers who successfully completed such details described being underutilized or, in some cases, being less competitive for promotion upon their return to DOS.[22] The State Department should encourage and support more details outside of the department to the National Security Council, Congress, the interagency, the United Nations, and the private sector; make these opportunities transparent for competition; and reward strong performance with greater responsibility and opportunity for advancement upon return.

A revolving door approach could also retain high-performing FSOs, particularly working parents, who choose to leave DOS mid-career for personal reasons, and allow a return to active duty within a fixed period (e.g., six years) at the same grade, with options for periodic recalls, to both meet surge needs and keep clearances and knowledge current. To remain a competitive employer and retain FSOs with parenting responsibilities, DOS also needs to address the extended work hours and undivided commitment that many Foreign and Civil Service positions demand, challenges identified by sociologists as common to the "greedy professions." Addressing them requires more attention to job sharing, rotational schedules, and teleworking, which has been implemented to an extent never imagined through the COVID-19 pandemic. Although gender-neutral on the surface, extended work and undivided attention have a gender dimension. Tellingly, only 6 percent of mothers currently work in jobs requiring a commitment of at least fifty hours per week relative to 20 percent of fathers.[23]

REBOOTING AND EXPANDING TRAINING AND CONTINUOUS LEARNING

State Department training is both undervalued and insufficient to produce a twenty-first-century workforce. Beyond three to six weeks of training for Foreign Service entry-level generalists and specialists, language training, and short leadership courses at mid- and senior levels, learning opportunities are insufficient for a diplomatic service, which is one of the few that does not require a college degree. Civil Service training is even less forthcoming beyond initial orientation and out of reach for most locally employed staff, who make up nearly 60 percent of the State Department workforce. A long tradition of on-the-job training produces an unhelpful mentality articulated in a recent *Foreign Service Journal* article that great officers are "born not made."[24] A parallel perception holds that long-term training could actually hurt FSOs' promotion potential by removing them from evaluations that are the basis for advancement in a time-bound "up or out" system. By comparison, other major diplomatic services invest two to three years of training before sending officers overseas, whereas most U.S. military officers must complete a year of advanced professional education or a civilian advanced degree to be competitive for senior ranks.[25]

With the Foreign Service Institute budget overwhelmingly devoted to language training, the State Department should take a harder look at how training resources are allocated and recruit more incoming officers with foreign language skills. For instance, Hispanic representation in the workforce is 60 percent below that of the U.S. population, while, according to the American Academy for Diplomacy, the State Department trains seven times more speakers in Spanish than there are Spanish-language-designated positions.[26] DOS still has more Portuguese speakers than Arabic and Chinese combined and more Albanian speakers than Urdu, Dari, or Farsi. Language-designated positions overseas are 15 percent vacant, and 24 percent of those staffed are filled by officers who do not meet the minimum language requirement.[27]

The State Department should affirm a commitment to continuing education by

- increasing staffing pipelines and funding to create a training float that will deepen officers' command of the fundamentals of diplomatic tradecraft, including policy development and doctrine, case studies, negotiation, crisis management, program management, and specialized knowledge throughout their career path;

- incentivizing continuous learning as a precept for promotion and rewarding managers for allowing their people to get training;

- increasing opportunities for mid-level Foreign and Civil Service officers to pursue long-term training and graduate study outside DOS in priority issue areas, with a target of mandatory long-term professional education for promotion to the Senior Foreign and Executive Service; and

- devoting greater attention to recruiting more officers with language skills, revising security policies that prevent heritage speakers from serving in their countries of origin, and requiring multiple assignments in language-designated positions for officers who receive FSI training.

One recently retired ambassador underscored training and education as integral to "lifting the dead hand of department institutional culture," setting the command environment, and creating a more resilient institution capable of structural reform and less vulnerable to political predation.[28]

BEYOND THE
NEAR TERM

The foregoing recommendations are intended as a road map for an administration from either major party to implement in 2021, requiring nothing more than decisions to be made by a secretary of state and without needing congressional action. But a new term or administration offers at least a four-year mandate, and American diplomacy and the State Department would also benefit from some longer-term thinking, even if those goals are more difficult to accomplish.

AMEND THE FOREIGN SERVICE ACT

The first is a new Foreign Service Act to replace the version most recently amended during the Carter administration. The Foreign Service Act of 1980, which established the State Department's inspector general and the Foreign Service union, strengthened oversight of diversity issues, and reduced the number of personnel categories, among other steps, has now been in force longer than either of its predecessors passed in 1924 and 1946. Some State Department champions have warned against reopening this legislation, concerned that an uncertain and polarized congressional environment would only make things worse. But at least one sound reason to pursue a new Foreign Service Act is to codify as many of the reforms recommended above as possible. This would make the State Department more durable and less vulnerable to the vagaries of a revisionist administration that could undo administrative actions as easily as they were taken. Further analysis of what such legislation could include, beyond the reforms recommended above, would be worth undertaking in future studies.

UNIFIED NATIONAL SECURITY BUDGETING

Although the annual National Defense Authorization Act—and the more than $700 billion it approves—is considered one of the few "must-pass" pieces of legislation, authorizing the roughly $50 billion State Department budget is exceedingly rare. The politics that produces this situation is one of many reasons the United States is often prone to a militarized foreign policy, with authorities, programs, and resources—particularly those related to security assistance—shifting from diplomacy to defense. As a result, a range of organizations—from the Task Force on a Unified Security Budget to the nongovernmental organization Win Without War to the State Department under Secretary Hillary Clinton—have proposed reforming the budgetary process to allow for unified consideration of all civilian and military functions in a single omnibus process. As one recent article advocating for such an approach argued, "There are a number of possible routes to consider—require cross-subcommittee hearings, create a new supercommittee, break up and merge existing authorization and appropriations committees—each of which would require different degrees of structural change."[29]

Resistance to such an approach is substantial, starting with the powerful chairs and ranking members of the House and Senate Armed Services Committees, who currently lord over perhaps the most important annual legislation on Capitol Hill, the National Defense Authorization Act. But if the country is serious about making diplomacy the most important foreign policy tool at its disposal, it should pay for it accordingly. This change could have the salutary effect of forcing the executive branch to think more comprehensively about national security priorities and the tools for advancing them, though enacting that change would require a broader effort to reform a budget process too often captured by more parochial political considerations and constituencies. Even absent the formal adoption of a unified budget, a mindset that rebalances resources expended on national security—and the authorities that attach to and flow from those resources—would be a welcome change.

DIPLOMATIC RESERVE CORPS

The State Department should establish a Diplomatic Reserve Corps, modeled on the military's Reserve Officers' Training Corps, through which citizens in other professions perform part-time military service and are occasionally deployed full time.[30] Ideally, such a cadre would be made up not of new college graduates or retirees but of experienced former Foreign and Civil Service mid-level officers and spouses with professional experience who would make themselves available to take on shorter or fixed-term assignments abroad and in Washington. The size and cost of such an endeavor could vary widely, but, with DOS Foreign and Civil Service numbering about 25,000 members, a reserve core of even 2,500, or 10 percent, would make a meaningful difference, at manageable cost. This surge capacity could help the State Department fill endemic vacancies overseas, support a long-sought training float to professionalize the career cadre at all stages, and address the recurrent retention problem of lack of spousal employment abroad.

CONCLUSION

The Department of State remains a world-class diplomatic institution that employs thousands of the U.S. government's most capable public servants. But left unaddressed, the challenges that DOS faces risk causing irreparable damage to America's standing and influence in the world, ability to advance its interests overseas, and security and prosperity at home. This means addressing deficiencies in DOS policy focus and capacity, institutional culture, and workforce diversity and flexibility, while laying the groundwork to cement these and other changes through legislation. Perhaps the biggest challenge to advancing this agenda will be the secretary of state's calculus about whether to make it a priority, given the inevitable policy debates and diplomatic crises that will occupy their time. Prioritizing reform, even in the face of competing demands, is among the most enduring contributions that could be made to American security and prosperity and is essential to equipping American diplomacy for the issues the country faces. Another challenge, particularly in an age in which so many governing approaches fail to outlast the next election cycle—even in a foreign affairs landscape that was once more insulated from political vagaries—will be making such reforms stick. Legislation to codify them would help but is neither guaranteed to pass nor, if it does, guaranteed to be implemented as intended. For this reason, the proposed cultural changes, bringing institutional weight to bear to prevent backsliding, are critical. But DOS should also make a strong public case for the proposed changes—reminding the American people of the important role diplomacy plays in their daily lives that should not be taken for granted. Building a constituency for diplomacy and diplomats—not unlike that which exists for U.S. military institutions and personnel—would be a worthwhile, if generational, project. In the meantime, an administration less hostile to diplomacy than the current can begin reversing the present crisis in its early days by implementing long-overdue changes under existing authorities. Transformation, not restoration, should be the secretary of state's mandate.

ENDNOTES

1. Neta C. Crawford, "United States Budgetary Costs and Obligations of Post-9/11 Wars Through FY2020: $6.4 Trillion," Watson Institute for International and Public Affairs, Brown University, November 13, 2019, http://watson.brown.edu/costsofwar/files/cow /imce/papers/2019/US%20Budgetary%20Costs%20of%20Wars%20November%20 2019.pdf; Task Force on Extremism in Fragile States, *Preventing Extremism in Fragile States: A New Approach* (Washington, DC: U.S. Institute of Peace, February 2019), http://usip.org/sites/default/files/2019-02/preventing-extremism-in-fragile-states-a -new-approach.pdf.

2. "Bureau of Economic and Business Affairs," U.S. Department of State, accessed July 2, 2020, http://state.gov/bureaus-offices/under-secretary-for-economic-growth-energy-and -the-environment/bureau-of-economic-and-business-affairs.

3. "State Department: Additional Steps Are Needed to Identify Potential Barriers to Diversity," U.S. Government Accountability Office, January 27, 2020, http://gao.gov /products/GAO-20-237.

4. Foreign Service Statistics, American Foreign Service Association, March 2020, http:// afsa.org/sites/default/files/0320_diversity_data_for_web.pdf.

5. Bureau of Human Resources, "Five-Year Workforce Plan: Fiscal Years 2019–2023," U.S. Department of State, February 2020, http://state.gov/wp-content/uploads/2020 /02/Five-Year-Workforce-Plan-FY19_FY23-Final.pdf.

6. Authors' conversations with former Pickering and Rangel fellows. All interviews were conducted in confidentiality, and the names of interviewees are withheld by mutual agreement.

7. "State Department: Minorities and Women Are Underrepresented in the Foreign Service," U.S. Government Accountability Office, June 26, 1989, http://gao.gov/assets /150/147826.pdf.

8. Paige Arthur, "The UN Strategy on Gender Parity," Center on International Cooperation, New York University, September 15, 2017, http://cic.nyu.edu/publications /un-strategy-gender-parity.

9. "Additional Steps Are Needed," Government Accountability Office.

10. Anne Woods Patterson, "We Have to Be There," *Foreign Service Journal*, September 2019, http://afsa.org/we-have-be-there.

11. Susan Cornwell, "Danger and Separation From Families Changing Job of U.S. Diplomats," Reuters, May 19, 2013, http://reuters.com/article/us-usa-diplomats /danger-and-separation-from-families-changing-job-of-u-s-diplomats -idUSBRE94I01G20130519.

12. Authors' conversation with former FSOs.

13. Office of Inspector General, "Audit of the U.S. Mission Iraq Staffing Process," U.S. Department of State, August 2013, http://stateoig.gov/system/files/214910.pdf.

14. "United States Department of State Professional Ethos," U.S. Department of State, accessed July 7, 2020, http://state.gov/about/professional-ethos.

15. Authors' conversation with a former senior FSO.

16. Bureau of Human Resources, "Five-Year Workforce and Leadership Succession Plan Fiscal Years 2018–2022," U.S. Department of State, February 2019, http://state.gov /wp-content/uploads/2019/05/Workforce-and-Leadership-Succession-Plan-FY18 _FY22-Final.pdf.

17. Dan De Luce, "Fewer Americans Are Opting for Careers at the State Department," NBC News, February 25, 2019, http://nbcnews.com/politics/national-security/fewer -americans-are-opting-careers-state-department-n973631.

18. Robbie Gramer, "At Embassies Abroad, Trump Envoys Are Quietly Pushing Out Career Diplomats," *Foreign Policy*, February 5, 2020, http://foreignpolicy.com/2020 /02/05/us-embassies-abroad-trump-envoys-pushing-out-career-diplomats-deputy -chiefs-mission-south-africa-diplomacy-pompeo-lana-marks.

19. Jory Heckman, "State Department Personnel Chief Sees Opportunities, Challenges With Less Experienced Workforce," *Federal News Network*, April 17, 2019, http:// federalnewsnetwork.com/workforce/2019/04/state-dept-personnel-chief-sees -opportunities-challenges-with-less-experienced-workforce.

20. "Advocacy Seminar," American Foreign Service Association, May 3, 2019, http://afsa .org/sites/default/files/advocacy-seminar-slides-050319.pdf.

21. Authors' conversations with former mid-level FSOs.

22. Authors' conversations with former FSOs.

23. Claire Cain Miller, "Women Did Everything Right. Then Work Got 'Greedy.'," *New York Times*, April 26, 2019, http://nytimes.com/2019/04/26/upshot/women-long -hours-greedy-professions.html.

24. Andrea Susana Martinez Donnally and Christina T. Le, "Breaking Away From 'Born, Not Made,'" *Foreign Service Journal*, April 2020, http://afsa.org/sites/default/files /flipping_book/0420/20/index.html.

25. Brent Scowcroft, "Forging a 21st-Century Diplomatic Service for the United States Through Professional Education and Training," Henry L. Stimson Center and American Academy of Diplomacy, February 2011, http://academyofdiplomacy.org /wp-content/uploads/2016/01/Forging-a-21st-Century-Diplomatic-Service-Full -Content.pdf; Susan D. Hosek, Peter Tiemeyer, M. Rebecca Kilburn, Debra A.

Strong, Selika Ducksworth, and Reginald Ray, "Description of an Officer's Career," in *Minority and Gender Differences in Officer Career Progression* (Santa Monica, CA: Rand Corporation, 2001), 7–24, http://rand.org/content/dam/rand/pubs/monograph _reports/MR1184/MR1184.ch2.pdf.

26. "Strengthening the Department of State," American Academy of Diplomacy, May 2019, http://academyofdiplomacy.org/wp-content/uploads/2019/05/AAD _Strengthening_the_State_web_version.pdf; Foreign Service Statistics, American Foreign Service Association; "QuickFacts: United States," U.S. Census Bureau, http:// census.gov/quickfacts/fact/table/US/RHI725218.

27. Bureau of Human Resources, "Five-Year Workforce Plan: Fiscal Years 2019–2023."

28. Authors' conversation with a former ambassador.

29. Brett Rosenberg and Jake Sullivan, "The Case for a National Security Budget," *Foreign Affairs*, November 19, 2019, http://foreignaffairs.com/articles/2019-11-19/case -national-security-budget.

30. Kori N. Schake and Brett McGurk, "Compete With China? Support a GI Bill for Diplomacy." *Washington Post*, May 13, 2019, http://washingtonpost.com/opinions /compete-with-china-support-a-gi-bill-for-diplomacy/2019/05/13/79823b80-7330 -11e9-8be0-ca575670e91c_story.html.

ABOUT THE AUTHORS

Uzra S. Zeya is the CEO and president of the Alliance for Peacebuilding, a network of more than 130 organizations working in over 180 countries to end conflict through peaceful means. She is also a board of advisors member at Georgetown University's Institute for the Study of Diplomacy. Zeya served as the chargé d'affaires and deputy chief of mission from 2014 to 2017 at the U.S. Embassy in Paris, where she led the U.S. response to three major terror attacks and forged unprecedented cooperation with France in combating terrorism in Africa and the Middle East, countering Russian aggression and malign influence in Europe, and mobilizing global action to confront climate change. Zeya previously served as acting assistant secretary and principal deputy assistant secretary in the Bureau of Democracy, Human Rights, and Labor from 2012 to 2014. As chief of staff to the deputy secretary of state from 2011 to 2012, she helped shape the U.S. policy response to the Arab Spring and deepened U.S. engagement with emerging powers. She also served as deputy executive secretary to Secretaries Condoleezza Rice and Hillary Clinton and overseas at embassies in New Delhi, Muscat, Damascus, Cairo, and Kingston. She is the recipient of the Legion of Honor, France's highest civilian honor, and fifteen superior honor and senior performance awards.

Jon Finer is adjunct senior fellow for U.S. foreign policy at the Council on Foreign Relations. He also oversees the political risk and public policy practice at Warburg Pincus LLC, a global investment firm. Previously, he was the chief of staff and director of policy planning at the State Department, serving as Secretary of State John Kerry's principal advisor and helping lead priority diplomatic initiatives, including the Iran nuclear negotiations and the Paris climate accord. Finer served in the White House during the first term of the Obama administration, starting as a White House fellow in the office of the chief of staff and also working as Vice President Joe Biden's Middle East advisor and foreign policy speech writer, as well as on the National Security Council staff. Before his time in government, Finer reported from more than a dozen countries as a foreign and national correspondent for the *Washington Post*, including covering the invasion of Iraq while embedded with the U.S. Marine Corps and spending eighteen months in Baghdad during the descent into civil war. He also covered conflicts in Georgia, Lebanon, and Gaza. He began his career at the *Far Eastern Economic Review*, a news and business magazine in Hong Kong. He is the cofounder and chair of the International Refugee Assistance Project, a nonresident advisor at the New York University Law School's Reiss Center for Law and Security, and a director of the Truman Center for National Policy.

ADVISORY COMMITTEE
Revitalizing the State Department and American Diplomacy

Daniel P. Benaim
Century Foundation

Virginia Bennett
CNA

Oni Blair
LINK Houston

Allyn Brooks-LaSure
Leadership Conference on Civil and Human Rights

William J. Burns, *Co-chair*
Carnegie Endowment for International Peace

Piper A. Campbell
American University

Sheba Crocker
CARE

Jeffrey DeLaurentis
Georgetown University

Dan Feldman
Covington & Burling LLP

Jeffrey D. Feltman
Brookings Institution

Alan Fitts
JPMorgan Chase & Co.

Michael E. Guest
Council for Global Equality

Grant T. Harris
Harris Africa Partners LLC

Jane Hartley
Carnegie Endowment for International Peace

Roberta S. Jacobson
Albright Stonebridge Group

Kay King

Harold H. Koh
Yale Law School

Prem J. Kumar
Albright Stonebridge Group

Barbara A. Leaf
Washington Institute for Near East Policy

Mark W. Lippert
YouTube

This report reflects the judgments and recommendations of the authors. It does not necessarily represent the views of members of the advisory committee, whose involvement should in no way be interpreted as an endorsement of the report by either themselves or the organizations with which they are affiliated.

Kelly E. Magsamen
Center for American Progress

Scott Nathan
Atlantic Neptune

Suzanne Nossel
PEN America

Sahar Nowrouzzadeh
*Belfer Center for Science
and International Affairs*

Jennifer Park Stout
Snap Inc.

Anne W. Patterson
Jackson Institute for Global Affairs

Michael Posner
NYU Stern School of Business

Joshua Rubin
Yale Law School

Daniel R. Russel
Asia Society

Thomas Shannon Jr.
Arnold & Porter

Dana Shell Smith
Georgetown University

Tara D. Sonenshine
Elliott School of International Affairs

Stephen Tankel
American University

Linda Thomas-Greenfield,
*Co-chair
Albright Stonebridge Group*

Kurt Tong
Asia Group LLC

Christopher M. Tuttle
Council on Foreign Relations

Earl Wayne
*Woodrow Wilson International Center
for Scholars*

Frank G. Wisner
Squire Patton Boggs

Zaid A. Zaid
Facebook

Ricardo Zuniga
*Woodrow Wilson International
Center for Scholars*

Made in the USA
Middletown, DE
29 March 2022